THE EXTRAORDINARY COMEDY OF RICKY GERVAIS

From Awkward Beginnings to Global Stardom, a Comedian's Unapologetic Journey to Challenge the Norms and Make the World Laugh

Paul C. Andrew

Copyright Page

Copyright **[2023] [PAUL C. ANDREW]**
All rights reserved. No part of this book may be reproduced in any form or by any electronic or mechanical means, including information storage and retrieval systems, without permission in writing from the publisher, except by a reviewer who may quote brief passages in a review.

The Information contained in this book is based on the author's experiences and research. The author has made every effort to provide accurate and up-to-date information, but makes no warranty or representation, express or implied, as to the accuracy or completeness of the information contained in this book. The author shall not be liable for any errors or omissions or for any actions taken based on the information contained in this book.

Table of Contents

Introduction

Chapter 1 Early Life and Background

Chapter 2 Stand-up Comedy and Hosting

Transition to Stand-up Comedy

Chapter 3 Podcasting and Broadcasting

The Ricky Gervais Podcast

Chapter 4 Writing and Publishing

Books and Essays

Chapter 5 Personal Life and Philanthropy

Relationships and Family

Introduction

In "THE EXTRAORDINARY LIFE AND COMEDY OF RICKY GERVAIS" we delve into the extraordinary journey of one of the most influential and unapologetic comedians of our time. From his humble beginnings to global stardom, Ricky Gervais has become a household name, pushing the boundaries of comedy and challenging societal norms with his unique blend of wit, satire, and unfiltered honesty.

This book takes you behind the scenes, offering an intimate and revealing portrait of Gervais' life and career. From his early experiences in stand-up comedy and his groundbreaking work on "The Office," to his iconic hosting gigs at award shows and his thought-provoking social commentary, we explore the triumphs, controversies, and personal moments that have shaped Gervais' extraordinary path.

Prepare to embark on a journey filled with laughter, candid anecdotes, and a glimpse into the mind of a comedic genius. Through in-depth interviews, behind-the-scenes stories, and personal reflections, "Unfiltered" captures the essence of Ricky Gervais — the man behind the laughter, the artist unafraid to challenge conventions, and the compassionate advocate for causes close to his heart.

Whether you're a die-hard fan or new to Gervais' work, this book offers a comprehensive and entertaining exploration of his life, from his early struggles and breakthrough moments to his enduring legacy and influence on comedy and entertainment. Get ready to discover the untold stories, the triumphs and setbacks, and the unfiltered truth behind the laughter.

Join us as we unravel the layers of Ricky Gervais, exploring the comedic brilliance, the personal journey, and the impact of one of the most influential figures in comedy. "Unfiltered: The Life and Laughs of Ricky Gervais" is a must-read for anyone seeking an intimate and insightful look into the life of a comedic icon. So, sit back, relax, and get ready to embark on a laughter-filled journey through the remarkable life of Ricky Gervais.

Chapter 1 Early Life and Background

Birth and Family

Ricky Gervais was born on June 25, 1961, in Reading, Berkshire, England. He was the youngest of four siblings, with two brothers and one sister. His father, Lawrence Raymond Gervais, worked as a laborer for the Whitley Pumphouse Company, and his mother, Eva Sophia Gervais (née House), was a homemaker.

Growing up in a working-class family, Gervais had a modest upbringing. His parents instilled in him a strong work ethic and values of honesty and integrity. While they may not have had much in terms of material wealth, Gervais often reflects on the love and support he received from his family during his formative years.

Childhood and Education

During his childhood, Gervais developed an early interest in the performing arts. He would often entertain his family and friends with humorous stories and impressions, showcasing his natural comedic talent from a young age. Gervais has fond memories of family gatherings where he would take center stage, delivering jokes and imitating celebrities.

Gervais attended Whitley Park Junior School and later Ashmead Comprehensive School, both located in Reading. While he wasn't particularly academically inclined, his wit and humor made him popular among his peers. Despite his love for comedy, Gervais initially pursued a different career path.

After completing his secondary education, Gervais enrolled in the University College London (UCL), where he studied philosophy. His interest in philosophy and his passion for exploring the human condition would later become evident in his work, as he often incorporates social commentary and introspective themes into his comedy.

Although Gervais graduated from UCL with a degree in philosophy, he realized that his true passion lay in the world of entertainment and comedy. This realization would set him on a path that would ultimately lead to his remarkable success in the entertainment industry.

The early years of Ricky Gervais' life and the influence of his family and childhood experiences played a significant role in shaping his comedic sensibilities and providing a foundation for his future endeavors. From his humble beginnings in Reading, Gervais would go on to become one of the most influential and beloved figures in comedy and entertainment.

Early Career and Breakthrough

Entry into Entertainment Industry

Ricky Gervais' entry into the entertainment industry was a gradual process that involved a combination of determination, perseverance, and a bit of luck. His journey began in the early 1980s when he decided to pursue a career in music.

Gervais formed a band called "Seona Dancing" with his university friend, Bill Macrae. They released a few singles, including "More to Lose" and "Bitter Heart," which garnered some attention but failed to achieve commercial success. Despite their music career not taking off as planned, Gervais gained valuable experience performing on stage and honing his skills as a performer.

Realizing that his true talent lay in comedy and writing, Gervais shifted his focus to stand-up comedy. He started performing at small venues in London, gradually building a reputation as a skilled and innovative comedian. His unique blend of observational humor, sharp wit, and unabashed honesty quickly won over audiences, and he began to gain recognition within the comedy circuit.

Gervais' breakthrough moment came when he was noticed by television producer and writer, Ash Atalla, who was impressed by his stand-up performances. Atalla invited Gervais to collaborate on a television pilot called "Golden Years." Although the show was not picked up for a full series, it marked Gervais' first foray into television and laid the groundwork for his future success.

Following the experience with "Golden Years," Gervais caught the attention of BBC executives who offered him the opportunity to create his own show. This led to the creation of "The Office," a groundbreaking sitcom that would catapult Gervais to global recognition.

"The Office," which premiered in 2001, depicted the mundane and often absurd world of office life through a mockumentary-style format. Gervais co-wrote and starred in the series as the cringe-inducing and socially awkward office manager, David Brent. The show's realistic portrayal of workplace dynamics, its dry humor, and Gervais' masterful performance resonated with audiences and critics alike.

"The Office" became an instant hit, receiving critical acclaim for its innovative storytelling, relatable characters, and satirical depiction of corporate culture. Gervais' portrayal of David Brent earned him widespread praise and numerous awards, including a Golden Globe for Best Actor in a Television Series - Musical or Comedy.

The success of "The Office" not only launched Gervais' career but also revolutionized the sitcom genre. Its unique documentary-style approach, complete with awkward silences and cringe-inducing moments, inspired a wave of similar shows and influenced the comedic landscape for years to come.

Ricky Gervais' entry into the entertainment industry, from his early music career to his breakthrough in stand-up comedy and the creation of "The Office," showcases his resilience, versatility, and undeniable talent. It was through these early experiences that Gervais honed his comedic skills and laid the foundation for his extraordinary success in the world of entertainment.

The Ricky Gervais Show

"The Ricky Gervais Show" originated as a radio program on London's Xfm station and later evolved into a wildly popular podcast. It featured Ricky Gervais, Stephen Merchant, and Karl Pilkington engaging in humorous and often absurd conversations that captivated audiences around the world.

The show's format revolved around the dynamic between the three hosts. Ricky Gervais, known for his quick wit and sharp comedic timing, served as the primary instigator of the discussions. Stephen Merchant, Gervais' long-time writing partner and friend, played the role of the rational and often bemused co-host. Karl Pilkington, a producer at Xfm who became an unlikely comedic sensation, brought his unique and often bizarre perspectives to the table.

"The Ricky Gervais Show" podcast gained immense popularity and achieved record-breaking download numbers. Its success can be attributed to the genuine chemistry between the hosts and the entertaining interplay of their contrasting personalities. The show featured a variety of topics, ranging from pop culture and current events to philosophical musings and absurd hypothetical scenarios.

One of the highlights of "The Ricky Gervais Show" was Karl Pilkington's eccentric insights and peculiar observations about the world. His offbeat perspectives and deadpan delivery became a recurring source of laughter for listeners. Pilkington's endearing naivety and hilarious misunderstandings often sparked spirited debates and humorous exchanges between Gervais and Merchant.

"The Ricky Gervais Show" podcast not only entertained audiences with its comedic banter but also showcased Gervais' skill as a storyteller and interviewer. Gervais was able to draw out amusing anecdotes and personal stories from both Merchant and Pilkington, creating a rich tapestry of humor and entertainment.

Due to its immense popularity, "The Ricky Gervais Show" podcast was adapted into an animated television series. The animated show brought the conversations to life, adding visual humor to the already hilarious dialogues. The television adaptation garnered critical acclaim and further expanded Gervais' reach as a comedic genius.

"The Ricky Gervais Show" stands as a testament to Gervais' comedic talent and ability to connect with audiences through his infectious humor. It showcased his knack for storytelling, his adeptness at eliciting laughter, and his unique ability to transform ordinary conversations into uproarious comedic gold. The show's success solidified Gervais' status as a comedy icon and paved the way for his subsequent achievements in the entertainment industry.

The Office and Global Recognition

"The Office" marked a significant turning point in Ricky Gervais' career, catapulting him to global recognition and cementing his status as a comedic powerhouse. The groundbreaking sitcom, co-created and co-written by Gervais and Stephen Merchant, achieved immense success and left an indelible mark on the comedy landscape.

Premiering in 2001, "The Office" depicted the daily lives of office employees at the fictional Wernham Hogg Paper Company, located in the mundane town of Slough. Shot in a mockumentary style, the series provided a realistic and often cringe-inducing portrayal of workplace dynamics and the quirks of its characters.

At the heart of the show was Gervais' iconic portrayal of David Brent, the bumbling and self-deluded office manager. Brent's desperate desire for popularity and recognition, coupled with his complete lack of self-awareness, made him an unforgettable character. Gervais' masterful performance captured both the comedic and tragic aspects of Brent, generating moments of laughter and empathy from viewers.

"The Office" struck a chord with audiences and critics alike, receiving widespread acclaim for its innovative storytelling, authentic characters, and sharp social commentary. The series successfully blended humor with moments of pathos, exploring themes of ambition, dissatisfaction, and the mundane nature of modern work life. Its realistic portrayal of office politics and interpersonal relationships resonated with viewers worldwide.

The critical success of "The Office" translated into numerous awards and accolades for Gervais and the show. Gervais received a Golden Globe for his performance as David Brent, and the series itself won multiple awards, including Golden Globes, BAFTAs, and Emmys. Its impact extended beyond the realm of television, influencing the comedy genre and inspiring countless adaptations in different countries.

The international success of "The Office" led to Gervais gaining widespread recognition and acclaim as a comedic genius. He became a household name, with his distinctive brand of humor and his portrayal of David Brent firmly etched in the public consciousness. Gervais' natural comedic timing, ability to blend humor with vulnerability, and willingness to push boundaries contributed to his rise as one of the most influential and respected figures in comedy.

In addition to the original UK version of "The Office," Gervais went on to serve as an executive producer for the highly successful American adaptation of the show, further solidifying his impact on the global comedy landscape. His involvement in both versions showcased his versatility and creative vision, bridging the gap between British and American humor.

"The Office" remains a landmark achievement in Gervais' career, representing a defining moment that propelled him to international fame and recognition. It not only showcased his comedic talent and writing prowess but also highlighted his ability to capture the essence of human behavior and deliver social commentary through laughter. The enduring legacy of "The Office" continues to influence comedy television and inspire future generations of comedians.

The Office and Success as a Writer
Concept and Development of The Office

The concept and development of "The Office" began with Ricky Gervais and Stephen Merchant, who shared a vision to create a realistic and comedic portrayal of office life. Drawing inspiration from their own experiences working in mundane office jobs, they set out to create a mockumentary-style sitcom that would resonate with audiences.

Gervais and Merchant envisioned a series that would capture the everyday frustrations, awkward interactions, and power dynamics that exist within a typical workplace. They aimed to create characters that were relatable, flawed, and fully realized, providing audiences with a glimpse into the lives of ordinary office employees.

To achieve this, Gervais and Merchant developed a documentary format that would provide a sense of authenticity and allow for improvisation within the scripted dialogue. This approach allowed the actors to inhabit their characters and bring a naturalistic quality to their performances.

The iconic setting of Wernham Hogg Paper Company in the unassuming town of Slough became the backdrop for the series. The choice of a paper company, a mundane and somewhat outdated industry, further accentuated the monotony and banality of office life.

Gervais was instrumental in shaping the central character of David Brent, the regional manager of Wernham Hogg. Brent became the embodiment of an inept and socially awkward boss, whose misguided attempts at humor and desire for popularity often led to cringe-inducing situations. Gervais' portrayal of Brent captured the delicate balance between comedy and tragedy, humanizing the character while also making him a source of ridicule.

The writing process for "The Office" involved a meticulous attention to detail, with Gervais and Merchant crafting finely-tuned scripts that blended humor with moments of uncomfortable silence and emotional depth. The dialogue was sharp, filled with witty one-liners, and infused with the distinctive comedic voice that would become a trademark of Gervais' work.

"The Office" received a green light from the BBC and premiered in 2001 with a six-episode first season. The show quickly garnered critical acclaim and a dedicated fanbase, attracting viewers with its fresh and innovative approach to comedy. Its success led to additional seasons and a two-part Christmas special that wrapped up the storylines and provided closure for the characters.

The concept and development of "The Office" demonstrated Gervais' and Merchant's ability to create a compelling and relatable world that resonated with audiences. Their attention to detail, commitment to authenticity, and skillful writing resulted in a sitcom that stood out for its realism, humor, and poignant commentary on human nature. "The Office" not only solidified Gervais' reputation as a brilliant writer but also laid the foundation for his subsequent success in the world of comedy and entertainment.

Characters and Impact

"The Office" featured a memorable ensemble cast of characters, each contributing to the show's success and leaving a lasting impact on viewers. The carefully crafted and brilliantly portrayed characters brought depth, humor, and relatability to the series, making it a standout in the realm of sitcoms.

David Brent (played by Ricky Gervais): David Brent, the bumbling and self-absorbed regional manager of Wernham Hogg, became one of the most iconic characters in television history. Gervais' portrayal of Brent, with his cringe-inducing behavior, desperate desire for popularity, and occasional moments of vulnerability, created a character that audiences simultaneously laughed at and empathized with.

Tim Canterbury (played by Martin Freeman): Tim, the affable and sarcastic salesman, served as the show's moral compass. His witty banter, unrequited love for receptionist Dawn, and deadpan humor added depth to the series. Tim's relatable experiences and aspirations resonated with viewers, making him a fan favorite.

Dawn Tinsley (played by Lucy Davis): Dawn, the kind-hearted and engaged receptionist, struggled with her own dreams and the mundanity of her job. Davis brought charm and vulnerability to the role, capturing the longing and quiet strength of her character.

Gareth Keenan (played by Mackenzie Crook): Gareth, the eccentric and overly bureaucratic assistant to the regional manager, provided comic relief with his peculiar habits and unwavering adherence to rules. Crook's portrayal of Gareth's idiosyncrasies and oddball personality added layers of humor to the show.

Keith Bishop (played by Ewen Macintosh): Keith, the lovable yet unmotivated warehouse worker, delivered deadpan one-liners and became a source of comic relief. Macintosh's understated performance created a character that viewers couldn't help but root for.

"The Office" had a profound impact on both the comedy genre and popular culture as a whole. Its innovative mockumentary format, blending documentary-style cinematography with scripted comedy, revolutionized sitcom storytelling. The show's realism and relatable characters resonated with audiences, who saw glimpses of their own workplaces in the humor and situations depicted on screen.

"The Office" also influenced the way comedy was approached in television, inspiring a wave of similar mockumentary-style series. Its unique brand of humor, characterized by cringe-worthy moments, awkward silences, and sharp observational comedy, became a hallmark of Gervais' work and influenced subsequent comedies.

The international success of "The Office" led to numerous adaptations in different countries, showcasing its enduring appeal and cultural impact. The American version of "The Office," adapted by Greg Daniels and starring Steve Carell, went on to become a massive hit, further solidifying the legacy of the original series and introducing it to a wider global audience.

Beyond its impact on the comedy landscape, "The Office" sparked conversations about workplace dynamics, corporate culture, and the pursuit of happiness in the modern world. It provided a platform for Gervais to explore deeper themes while making audiences laugh, showcasing his ability to blend comedy with social commentary.

The characters of "The Office" and their impact on popular culture are a testament to Gervais' and the cast's talent for creating compelling, relatable, and enduringly funny characters. The show's legacy continues to resonate, with viewers discovering and appreciating its timeless humor and memorable characters long after its initial run.

Awards and Critical Acclaim

"The Office" garnered widespread critical acclaim and received numerous awards and nominations for its groundbreaking writing, performances, and innovative approach to sitcom storytelling. The series was recognized for its sharp humor, realistic portrayal of office life, and its ability to balance comedy with moments of genuine emotion.

Awards and accolades bestowed upon "The Office" include:

- Golden Globe Awards: "The Office" won the prestigious Golden Globe for Best Television Series - Musical or Comedy in 2004. Additionally, Ricky Gervais received a Golden Globe for Best Actor in a Television Series - Musical or Comedy for his portrayal of David Brent.

- British Academy Television Awards (BAFTA): The show was honored with two BAFTA Television Awards for Best Situation Comedy in 2002 and 2003. Ricky Gervais also received the BAFTA for Best Comedy Performance in 2002.

- Primetime Emmy Awards: "The Office" received three Primetime Emmy Awards, including Outstanding Comedy Series in 2006, and two for Outstanding Writing for a Comedy Series in 2006 and 2007.

- Writers Guild of America Awards: The series earned a Writers Guild of America Award for Television - Episodic Comedy in 2003.

- Royal Television Society Awards: "The Office" received several Royal Television Society Awards, including Best Situation Comedy and Best Writer - Comedy in 2001, and Best Situation Comedy Performance for Ricky Gervais in 2002.

In addition to these major awards, "The Office" received numerous other nominations and accolades, solidifying its place as one of the most celebrated sitcoms of its time.

The critical acclaim for "The Office" was resounding. Critics praised its unique mockumentary format, its honest and relatable characters, and its ability to find humor in the mundane aspects of everyday life. The series was lauded for its sharp writing, blending satire, observational humor, and moments of genuine pathos. Audiences and critics alike found themselves captivated by the show's ability to elicit both laughter and reflection.

"The Office" not only achieved commercial success but also had a profound cultural impact. It redefined the sitcom genre, inspiring countless imitations and adaptations around the world. Its influence can be seen in the rise of mockumentary-style comedies that followed in its footsteps.

The awards and critical acclaim bestowed upon "The Office" validated its status as a groundbreaking and influential television series. The show's ability to combine laughter, poignancy, and social commentary in a relatable and authentic way solidified Ricky Gervais' position as a leading figure in the comedy world and further established his reputation as a visionary writer and performer.

Chapter 2 Stand-up Comedy and Hosting

Transition to Stand-up Comedy

Ricky Gervais' transition to stand-up comedy marked another significant milestone in his career, showcasing his versatility as a performer and his skill in engaging audiences with his unique brand of humor. While Gervais had gained recognition for his work in television and radio, it was in the realm of stand-up comedy where he truly flourished.

After the success of "The Office," Gervais embarked on a career as a stand-up comedian, drawing upon his wit, observational skills, and sharp comedic timing to create a distinct style that resonated with audiences. His transition to stand-up allowed him to showcase his talents as a solo performer, captivating audiences with his energetic stage presence and his ability to tackle a wide range of topics with biting humor.

Gervais' stand-up routines often incorporated personal anecdotes, social commentary, and a healthy dose of self-deprecating humor. He fearlessly tackled controversial and taboo subjects, challenging societal norms and pushing boundaries in pursuit of laughter. Gervais' unique perspective and unapologetic approach to comedy won him a loyal fan base and further solidified his reputation as a fearless and uncompromising comedian.

One of Gervais' most notable stand-up shows is "Animals," which was recorded in 2003 and released as a stand-up special. In "Animals," Gervais explored topics such as religion, humanity's place in the animal kingdom, and the absurdities of modern life. The show received critical acclaim and showcased Gervais' ability to deliver sharp social commentary with a dose of irreverence and humor.

Gervais continued to tour and perform stand-up shows, releasing several stand-up specials that further established his presence in the comedy world. Notable specials include "Politics" (2004), "Fame" (2007), "Science" (2010), and "Humanity" (2018). Through his stand-up performances, Gervais demonstrated his ability to connect with audiences on a personal level, using humor as a vehicle to explore complex topics and challenge societal norms.

Beyond his work as a stand-up comedian, Gervais has also hosted several high-profile award shows, including the Golden Globe Awards. Known for his sharp wit and fearless approach to comedy, Gervais' hosting gigs have garnered both praise and controversy. His hosting style often involves delivering biting monologues, skewering celebrities and the industry with his trademark irreverence. Gervais' hosting stints have become highly anticipated events, attracting attention for his fearless roasting and no-holds-barred approach.

Ricky Gervais' transition to stand-up comedy showcased his ability to command the stage, engage audiences, and deliver his unique brand of humor with impeccable timing. His success as a stand-up comedian further solidified his status as a multi-talented entertainer and reinforced his reputation as a comedic force to be reckoned with.

Stand-up Specials and Tours

Ricky Gervais has delighted audiences around the world with his hilarious and thought-provoking stand-up comedy specials. Known for his sharp wit, fearless delivery, and unfiltered observations, Gervais has released a number of critically acclaimed stand-up specials and embarked on successful tours, solidifying his position as one of the most respected and popular comedians of his generation.

Some of Gervais' notable stand-up specials include:

- "Animals" (2003): Gervais' first solo stand-up special, "Animals," showcased his distinctive comedic style and tackled a range of topics, including religion, morality, and the human condition. The special garnered critical acclaim and further established Gervais as a formidable stand-up comedian.

- "Politics" (2004): In "Politics," Gervais delved into political and social issues with his trademark biting humor. The special featured Gervais' razor-sharp insights on topics such as war, terrorism, and the foibles of politicians. It demonstrated his ability to tackle controversial subjects while eliciting laughter and provoking thought.

- "Fame" (2007): "Fame" saw Gervais explore the absurdities and pitfalls of fame and celebrity culture. With his self-deprecating humor and no-holds-barred commentary, Gervais offered a satirical take on the world of celebrity and the pursuit of fame. The special received widespread acclaim for its sharp social critique and hilarious anecdotes.

- "Science" (2010): With "Science," Gervais continued his tradition of fearless and intelligent comedy. The special covered a wide range of topics, including atheism, the nature of belief, and the wonders of science. Gervais' ability to tackle complex subjects with humor and insight was on full display, earning him critical praise.

- "Humanity" (2018): Gervais' most recent stand-up special, "Humanity," delved into topics such as social media, offense culture, and the complexities of being human. The special showcased Gervais' ability to provoke thought and challenge societal norms, all while delivering his signature irreverent and hilarious commentary.

In addition to his stand-up specials, Gervais has embarked on successful comedy tours, entertaining audiences across the globe. His tours have included sold-out shows at renowned venues and festivals, where fans eagerly anticipate his sharp wit and unfiltered observations.

Gervais' stand-up comedy specials and tours have not only delighted audiences but also received critical acclaim for their humor, intelligence, and fearless approach. His ability to tackle controversial subjects, challenge societal norms, and provoke thought while keeping audiences entertained has cemented his reputation as one of the most influential and respected comedians of his time.

Whether through his stand-up specials or live performances on tour, Ricky Gervais continues to captivate audiences with his unique brand of comedy, showcasing his unrivaled talent for blending humor, social commentary, and thought-provoking insights.

Hosting Awards Shows

In addition to his successful career as a comedian, writer, and actor, Ricky Gervais has become renowned for his memorable and often controversial hosting gigs at prestigious awards shows. Known for his fearless and irreverent style, Gervais has brought his biting humor and no-holds-barred approach to some of the industry's most high-profile events, leaving a lasting impact on the awards show landscape.

Gervais first gained attention as a host when he took the stage at the 67th Golden Globe Awards in 2010. His sharp and controversial opening monologue, which targeted A-list celebrities and the industry itself, became the talk of the town. Gervais' irreverent jokes and willingness to skewer Hollywood's elite garnered both praise and criticism, making the Golden Globe Awards a must-watch event.

Following his initial success, Gervais was invited back to host the Golden Globe Awards in 2011, 2012, and 2016. Each time, he pushed boundaries and courted controversy with his unfiltered remarks and biting humor. Gervais' hosting gigs became highly anticipated events, with audiences tuning in to see which celebrities would be on the receiving end of his comedic jabs.

Gervais' hosting style is characterized by his fearless approach to comedy, taking aim at celebrities, industry practices, and cultural issues. His irreverence and willingness to challenge societal norms have made his hosting performances both entertaining and polarizing.

While hosting awards shows, Gervais has used his platform to address controversial topics and speak out on issues close to his heart. He has raised awareness about animal rights, criticized political and social hypocrisy, and advocated for freedom of speech. Gervais' ability to inject social commentary into his hosting duties has further solidified his status as a comedic provocateur.

Gervais' hosting gigs have extended beyond the Golden Globe Awards. In 2020, he hosted the 77th Golden Globe Awards for the fifth time, once again making headlines with his acerbic monologue and unapologetic humor. His hosting appearances have become an integral part of awards show history, often generating buzz and sparking discussions long after the event has ended.

Ricky Gervais' hosting style may not be for everyone, as his provocative and unfiltered approach has drawn both praise and criticism. However, there is no denying his impact on the awards show landscape. His willingness to challenge the status quo and push boundaries has breathed new life into these events, injecting them with a dose of edgy humor and controversy.

Gervais' hosting performances have redefined what it means to be an awards show host, proving that comedy can be a powerful tool for commentary, satire, and challenging the establishment. Whether loved or loathed, Gervais has left an indelible mark on the world of awards show hosting, cementing his reputation as an irreverent and unforgettable presence on stage.

Acting Career and Filmography

Acting Roles and Collaborations

Ricky Gervais has demonstrated his versatility as an actor through a range of roles in both film and television. Known for his ability to seamlessly transition between comedic and dramatic performances, Gervais has collaborated with acclaimed directors and talented actors, showcasing his talent and expanding his presence in the entertainment industry.

One of Gervais' notable acting collaborations is with director and writer Stephen Merchant. The duo co-created and starred in the critically acclaimed sitcom "The Office," where Gervais portrayed the iconic character David Brent. The success of "The Office" not only launched Gervais' career but also established him as a gifted actor and writer.

Following the success of "The Office," Gervais continued to pursue acting roles in film and television. Some of his notable film appearances include:

- "Ghost Town" (2008): In this romantic comedy, Gervais played the lead role of Bertram Pincus, a dentist who gains the ability to see ghosts. Gervais showcased his comedic timing and charm in this heartwarming and humorous film.

- "The Invention of Lying" (2009): Gervais co-wrote, co-directed, and starred in this satirical comedy. Set in a world where lying doesn't exist, Gervais' character Mark Bellison discovers the power of deception. The film allowed Gervais to explore his comedic and writing talents in a unique and thought-provoking way.

- "Night at the Museum" series (2006-2014): Gervais appeared in multiple installments of this adventure-comedy film franchise, playing the role of Dr. McPhee, the director of the Natural History Museum.

His dry wit and comedic timing added a memorable touch to the ensemble cast.

In addition to his film roles, Gervais has also made notable appearances on television. Some of his noteworthy television performances include:

- "Extras" (2005-2007): Gervais co-created and starred in this critically acclaimed sitcom, playing the role of Andy Millman, an aspiring actor. The series showcased Gervais' talent for blending comedy with poignant and reflective moments, earning him widespread praise.

- "Derek" (2012-2014): Gervais wrote, directed, and starred in this comedy-drama series. He portrayed the title character Derek Noakes, a kind-hearted caretaker in a nursing home. Gervais' nuanced performance in this touching and thought-provoking series earned him critical acclaim and showcased his range as an actor.

Gervais' acting collaborations extend beyond his own projects. He has appeared in films such as "Cemetery Junction" (2010), directed by Stephen Merchant and co-written by Gervais, and "Muppets Most Wanted" (2014), where he had a memorable supporting role.

Throughout his acting career, Ricky Gervais has demonstrated his ability to immerse himself in diverse roles, delivering performances that are both hilarious and heartfelt. Whether through his own creative ventures or collaborations with other talented individuals, Gervais continues to leave his mark on the entertainment industry as a versatile and respected actor.

Film and Television Projects

Ricky Gervais has been involved in a variety of film and television projects throughout his career, showcasing his talents as a writer, actor, and director. From critically acclaimed sitcoms to thought-provoking films, Gervais has left an indelible mark on the entertainment industry with his unique comedic style and ability to tackle complex subjects with humor and insight.

Here are some of the notable film and television projects that Ricky Gervais has been a part of:

- "The Office" (2001-2003):

Co-created and starring Ricky Gervais, "The Office" is a mockumentary-style sitcom that follows the daily lives of office employees. Gervais played the central character David Brent, a cringe-worthy and self-deluded office manager. The show gained international acclaim and has been regarded as one of the greatest sitcoms of all time.

- "Extras" (2005-2007):

Co-created and starring Ricky Gervais, "Extras" is a sitcom that follows the life of Andy Millman, an aspiring actor working as an extra. The show offers a satirical look at the entertainment industry and features cameo appearances from various celebrities playing exaggerated versions of themselves. "Extras" received critical acclaim for its clever writing and Gervais' performance.

- "Ghost Town" (2008):

In this romantic comedy film, Gervais stars as Bertram Pincus, a dentist who gains the ability to see ghosts after a near-death experience. As Pincus navigates the supernatural world, he finds himself entangled in a love triangle. Gervais' performance blends humor with heartfelt moments, adding depth to the character.

- "The Invention of Lying" (2009):

Co-written and co-directed by Ricky Gervais, "The Invention of Lying" is a satirical comedy set in a world where lying doesn't exist. Gervais plays the lead role of Mark Bellison, who discovers the ability to lie and uses it to his advantage. The film explores themes of truth, religion, and human nature through Gervais' trademark wit and observational humor.

- "Derek" (2012-2014):

Created, written, directed, and starring Ricky Gervais, "Derek" is a comedy-drama series that follows the life of Derek Noakes, a kind-hearted caretaker in a nursing home. Gervais delivers a poignant and sensitive performance, addressing themes of aging, compassion, and the importance of human connection.

- "Special Correspondents" (2016):

Written and directed by Ricky Gervais, "Special Correspondents" is a satirical comedy film that follows two radio journalists who fake war reports from a hideout instead of actually being on the front lines. Gervais' witty writing and comedic timing shine through in this clever and entertaining film.

These are just a few examples of the film and television projects in which Ricky Gervais has been involved. His work spans various genres, showcasing his versatility as a writer, actor, and director. Gervais' projects have garnered critical acclaim, entertained audiences worldwide, and solidified his reputation as a comedic talent with a knack for thought-provoking storytelling.

Notable Performances and Awards

Ricky Gervais has delivered numerous notable performances throughout his career, earning him critical acclaim and recognition in the entertainment industry. Known for his sharp wit, impeccable comedic timing, and ability to tackle complex subjects, Gervais has garnered accolades for his work in both television and film. Here are some of his notable performances and awards:

- David Brent in "The Office":

Gervais' portrayal of David Brent in the original UK version of "The Office" is considered one of his most iconic roles. His portrayal of the cringe-worthy and delusional office manager earned him widespread praise and established him as a talented actor. Gervais received numerous awards for his performance, including the British Academy Television Award for Best Comedy Performance.

- Andy Millman in "Extras":

In the sitcom "Extras," Gervais played the role of Andy Millman, an aspiring actor working as an extra. His performance in the series earned him critical acclaim and several accolades, including a Golden Globe Award for Best Actor in a Television Series – Musical or Comedy.

- Bertram Pincus in "Ghost Town":

Gervais' performance as Bertram Pincus, a dentist who gains the ability to see ghosts, in the romantic comedy film "Ghost Town" was well-received by both critics and audiences. His portrayal showcased his comedic talent and earned him a nomination for the Golden Globe Award for Best Actor in a Motion Picture – Musical or Comedy.

- Mark Bellison in "The Invention of Lying":

In the satirical comedy film "The Invention of Lying," Gervais played the lead role of Mark Bellison, a man who discovers the power of lying in a world where everyone tells the truth. Gervais' performance demonstrated his ability to blend humor with deeper themes, and he received praise for his portrayal of the complex character.

- Derek Noakes in "Derek":

Gervais wrote, directed, and starred in the comedy-drama series "Derek," where he played the title character. His performance as Derek Noakes, a kind-hearted caretaker in a nursing home, showcased his dramatic range and earned him critical acclaim. Gervais received multiple nominations for his work in the series, including a Golden Globe Award nomination for Best Actor in a Television Series – Drama.

In addition to his performances, Ricky Gervais has been recognized for his contributions to the entertainment industry with various awards and honors. Some of the notable accolades he has received include:

Seven British Academy Television Awards
Three Golden Globe Awards
Two Emmy Awards
A Rose d'Or Award
A Writers' Guild of Great Britain Award
These awards and honors reflect Gervais' impact and influence as a talented performer, writer, and comedian. His ability to captivate audiences with his comedic genius, coupled with his willingness to push boundaries and challenge conventions, has earned him a well-deserved place among the industry's most respected and celebrated talents.

Chapter 3 Podcasting and Broadcasting

The Ricky Gervais Podcast

In addition to his work in television and film, Ricky Gervais has made a significant impact in the world of podcasting and broadcasting. One of his most notable endeavors in this realm is "The Ricky Gervais Podcast," which became a groundbreaking and immensely popular audio series.

"The Ricky Gervais Podcast" originated from Gervais' earlier collaboration with Stephen Merchant and Karl Pilkington on their radio show on London's XFM. The trio's chemistry and unique dynamic led to the creation of the podcast, which was initially released in 2005.

The podcast format allowed Gervais, Merchant, and Pilkington to engage in candid and often hilarious conversations about various topics. At the center of the podcast was Karl Pilkington, who quickly became a fan favorite due to his distinctive perspectives and comedic musings. Gervais and Merchant would often tease and engage in playful banter with Pilkington, resulting in many memorable and laugh-out-loud moments.

"The Ricky Gervais Podcast" gained widespread popularity, attracting millions of listeners worldwide. The success of the podcast led to a Guinness World Record for the most downloaded podcast, reflecting its immense impact and influence on the medium.

The unique charm of the podcast came from the blend of Gervais' comedic prowess, Merchant's wit, and Pilkington's offbeat and unconventional observations. The trio's discussions covered a wide range of topics, including philosophy, science, and pop culture. Their unfiltered and humorous approach resonated with audiences and helped establish the podcast as a groundbreaking and influential show.

The success of "The Ricky Gervais Podcast" led to further collaborations between Gervais, Merchant, and Pilkington. They went on to create additional podcast series, including "The Ricky Gervais Guide to..." and "The Karl Pilkington Podcast," which continued to captivate audiences with their humor and unique insights.

The impact of "The Ricky Gervais Podcast" extended beyond the audio format. The popularity of the podcast paved the way for other comedians and entertainers to explore podcasting as a medium, contributing to the rise of podcasting as a mainstream form of entertainment.

Ricky Gervais' foray into podcasting not only showcased his ability to entertain and engage audiences through audio content but also solidified his status as a pioneer in the podcasting landscape. His unique approach to conversation, combined with the comedic chemistry between him, Stephen Merchant, and Karl Pilkington, left an indelible mark on the podcasting industry and contributed to its widespread popularity and success.

Radio Shows and Podcasting Success

Ricky Gervais has achieved remarkable success in the realm of radio shows and podcasting, utilizing these mediums to connect with audiences and further showcase his comedic talents and engaging personality. From radio broadcasts to highly popular podcasts, Gervais has cemented his status as a pioneer in the audio entertainment landscape.

Early in his career, Gervais co-hosted a radio show on London's XFM alongside his creative partner, Stephen Merchant. The radio show provided a platform for Gervais and Merchant to showcase their witty banter, humorous observations, and irreverent comedic style. The duo's radio broadcasts gained a loyal following and laid the foundation for their future collaborations.

Building on the success of their radio show, Gervais, Merchant, and Karl Pilkington ventured into the world of podcasting, resulting in the creation of "The Ricky Gervais Podcast." The podcast retained the format of their radio show, allowing Gervais, Merchant, and Pilkington to engage in candid and often hilarious conversations about various topics.

"The Ricky Gervais Podcast" quickly gained traction and became a groundbreaking success. The podcast's blend of humor, intellectual discussions, and the unique perspective of Karl Pilkington captivated audiences worldwide. It became one of the most downloaded podcasts of all time, setting a Guinness World Record and paving the way for the mainstream acceptance and popularity of podcasts.

Gervais' podcasting success continued with subsequent projects, such as "The Ricky Gervais Guide to..." and "The Karl Pilkington Podcast." These audio series further showcased Gervais' ability to entertain and engage listeners through captivating conversations and humorous dialogues.

In addition to his own podcasts, Gervais has appeared as a guest on various popular podcasts, engaging in interviews and discussions with fellow podcast hosts. His appearances on podcasts have allowed him to reach new audiences and further solidify his presence in the podcasting realm.

Gervais' success in radio shows and podcasting has been fueled by his natural comedic talent, sharp wit, and ability to connect with audiences on an intimate level. His podcasts have provided a platform for his unique brand of humor, intellectual musings, and thought-provoking discussions, showcasing his versatility and creativity beyond traditional media formats.

Moreover, Gervais' accomplishments in podcasting have helped to elevate the medium itself, playing a pivotal role in the growth and mainstream recognition of podcasts as a form of entertainment. His contributions have inspired countless comedians, entertainers, and creators to explore the possibilities of podcasting, contributing to its continued popularity and cultural significance.

Through his radio shows and podcasts, Ricky Gervais has solidified his place as a trailblazer in the audio entertainment landscape. His comedic genius, engaging presence, and groundbreaking success have made a lasting impact, leaving an indelible mark on the world of radio broadcasting and podcasting.

Contributions to Broadcasting

Ricky Gervais has made significant contributions to the field of broadcasting throughout his career. His unique comedic style, thought-provoking content, and willingness to push boundaries have not only entertained audiences but also influenced and shaped the landscape of broadcasting.

- Innovation in Comedy:

Gervais is known for his innovative approach to comedy, challenging traditional comedic conventions and pushing boundaries. His groundbreaking sitcom "The Office" revolutionized the mockumentary format, introducing a new style of storytelling that blurred the line between reality and fiction. This innovative approach influenced a generation of comedians and writers, reshaping the comedic landscape in television and broadcasting.

- Social Commentary and Satire:

Gervais is renowned for his ability to use humor as a tool for social commentary and satire. Through projects like "The Office" and "Extras," he addressed societal issues, challenged social norms, and provided incisive commentary on topics such as workplace dynamics, celebrity culture, and the pursuit of fame. Gervais' satire often exposes the absurdities of human behavior, inviting audiences to reflect on their own lives and society as a whole.

- Influence on Comedy Writing:

Gervais' unique writing style has had a profound impact on the field of comedy writing. His use of cringe humor, dry wit, and observational comedy has influenced countless writers and comedians, shaping the comedic landscape in both television and film. The success of his projects, such as "The Office" and "Extras," has demonstrated the power of sharp writing and authentic characters, leading to a shift in comedic storytelling.

Hosting Awards Shows:

Gervais has become a sought-after host for awards shows, bringing his sharp comedic sensibility and irreverent humor to prestigious events. His hosting appearances at the Golden Globe Awards, in particular, have garnered significant attention and acclaim. Gervais' unapologetic and often controversial monologues have challenged the status quo and injected a fresh, provocative energy into the awards show circuit.

- Podcasting and Broadcasting Pioneering:

With the success of "The Ricky Gervais Podcast" and subsequent podcasting projects, Gervais has played a pivotal role in popularizing podcasting as a mainstream form of entertainment. His podcasting success has paved the way for other comedians and entertainers to explore the medium, leading to a boom in podcast creation and consumption. Gervais' contributions to podcasting have revolutionized the broadcasting landscape, providing a new platform for creative expression and engaging storytelling.

Ricky Gervais' contributions to broadcasting go beyond mere entertainment. Through his innovative approach, social commentary, and influence on comedy writing, he has left an indelible mark on the field. His willingness to challenge conventions and tackle controversial topics has shaped the way comedy is perceived and appreciated, while his ventures into podcasting have contributed to the evolution and democratization of broadcasting as a whole.

Chapter 4 Writing and Publishing

Books and Essays

In addition to his success in television, film, and broadcasting, Ricky Gervais has made notable contributions to the world of writing and publishing. Known for his wit and insightful observations, Gervais has authored books and essays that showcase his unique comedic voice and offer readers a deeper understanding of his thoughts and perspectives.

Gervais has published several books throughout his career, including both fiction and non-fiction works. Here are some of his notable books:

- "Flanimals" Series:

"Flanimals" is a series of illustrated books written by Gervais, featuring bizarre and imaginative creatures that he created. These humorous and whimsical books not only showcase Gervais' creativity but also offer a satirical commentary on human behavior and societal norms.

- "The World of Karl Pilkington":

In collaboration with Karl Pilkington, Gervais co-authored "The World of Karl Pilkington," a collection of humorous writings that revolve around Pilkington's unique perspectives on various topics. The book provides an intimate look into Pilkington's unconventional and often hilarious take on the world.

- "Ricky Gervais Presents: The World of Karl Pilkington":

Building on their successful podcasting ventures, Gervais and Pilkington published a book that compiled transcripts from their podcast episodes. This book captures the essence of their comedic chemistry and allows readers to delve into their entertaining conversations.

In addition to his book publications, Gervais has also written essays and articles that touch on a wide range of subjects. These writings offer readers a glimpse into his thoughts on comedy, atheism, social issues, and more. Gervais' essays often exhibit his sharp wit and critical thinking, sparking discussions and provoking thought among readers.

Gervais' writing style is characterized by his ability to blend humor with astute observations about the human condition. Whether he is exploring the absurdities of everyday life, delving into philosophical questions, or challenging societal norms, his writings captivate readers with his unique perspective and comedic sensibilities.

Furthermore, Gervais' success as an author and essayist reflects his versatility as a creative talent. His ability to engage and entertain audiences through the written word showcases his skill as a storyteller and his commitment to exploring different mediums of artistic expression.

Ricky Gervais' books and essays not only provide entertainment but also offer readers an opportunity to delve deeper into his comedic genius and gain insights into his thoughts and views on various topics. Through his writing and publishing endeavors, Gervais continues to leave a lasting impact, captivating audiences with his humor and thought-provoking content.

Autobiography and Memoirs

Ricky Gervais has shared his life experiences, reflections, and insights through his autobiography and memoirs. These books offer readers a personal and intimate look into his journey, shedding light on the influences, challenges, and successes that have shaped his career and personal life.

- "Flanimals of the Deep" (2006):
While not strictly an autobiography or memoir, "Flanimals of the Deep" is worth mentioning as it provides readers with a glimpse into Gervais' creative mind. The book continues the "Flanimals" series, introducing a new collection of bizarre and fantastical creatures with humorous descriptions and illustrations.

- "The Ricky Gervais Guide to...":
As part of a series of audiobooks, Gervais released "The Ricky Gervais Guide to..." in collaboration with Stephen Merchant and Karl Pilkington. Although not traditional autobiographical works, these guides feature humorous conversations and anecdotes, giving listeners insights into the trio's personal dynamics and shared experiences.

- "Flanimals: The Day of the Bletchling" (2007):
Continuing the "Flanimals" series, "The Day of the Bletchling" features more of Gervais' imaginative creations, accompanied by witty descriptions and

illustrations. While not focused on his personal life, these books offer a glimpse into Gervais' creativity and humor.

- "Ricky Gervais Presents: The World of Karl Pilkington" (2009): Co-authored with Karl Pilkington, this book compiles their conversations from the podcast episodes, providing readers with an entertaining and amusing look into their dynamic and Pilkington's peculiar worldview.

- "Ricky Gervais: The Story So Far" (2010): This autobiography provides a comprehensive account of Gervais' life and career up to that point. From his early days in stand-up comedy to the creation of "The Office" and beyond, Gervais reflects on his journey, offering personal anecdotes and behind-the-scenes stories. The book delves into his influences, successes, and challenges, providing readers with a deeper understanding of his rise to fame.

- "More Flanimals" (2012): Continuing the "Flanimals" series, "More Flanimals" presents a fresh collection of whimsical creatures created by Gervais. These books showcase his creative and imaginative storytelling abilities, inviting readers into his fantastical world of bizarre beings.

Gervais' autobiography and memoirs allow readers to explore his personal and professional life through his own words. From his comedic influences and creative processes to his experiences in the entertainment industry, these books provide a deeper insight into the man behind the laughter.

Through his writings, Gervais shares his unique perspectives, anecdotes, and lessons learned, offering readers a chance to connect with him on a more personal level. His candid and often humorous storytelling style creates an engaging reading experience, allowing fans to further appreciate his journey and the experiences that have shaped him as a comedian and entertainer.

Ricky Gervais' autobiography and memoirs provide a valuable addition to his body of work, allowing readers to gain a deeper understanding of his life, career, and the creative forces that have shaped him into one of the most influential comedic voices of our time.

Literary Accomplishments

Ricky Gervais, while primarily known for his work in television, film, and comedy, has also made notable literary accomplishments throughout his career. From writing books to contributing to publications, Gervais has demonstrated his skill as a writer beyond the realm of performing.

- Books:

Gervais has authored several books that showcase his wit, humor, and unique storytelling ability. His "Flanimals" series, which features whimsical and absurd creatures accompanied by humorous descriptions and illustrations, has gained popularity among both children and adults. The books blend Gervais' creativity with his signature comedic style, offering a delightful reading experience.

- Essays and Articles:

Gervais has also written essays and articles on various topics, showcasing his sharp observations and thought-provoking insights. He has contributed to publications such as The Guardian, The Huffington Post, and The Wall Street Journal, offering his perspectives on subjects ranging from comedy and atheism to social issues and animal rights. Gervais' essays demonstrate his ability to combine humor with astute observations, engaging readers and encouraging them to think critically about the world around them.

- Awards and Recognition:

Gervais' literary accomplishments have not gone unnoticed. His "Flanimals" series, in addition to being commercially successful, has received critical acclaim and garnered awards. Gervais' books have been praised for their imaginative concepts, clever humor, and innovative approach to children's literature. The widespread recognition of his literary work further solidifies his status as a multi-talented entertainer and creative force.

- Contributions to Comedy Writing:

While not strictly literary in the traditional sense, Gervais' contributions to comedy writing have had a significant impact on the field. His creation of "The Office" and "Extras" showcased his ability to craft compelling and nuanced characters, write sharp and humorous dialogue, and navigate the complexities of human relationships. Gervais' skill as a writer has not only entertained audiences but has also influenced and inspired a new generation of comedy writers.

Ricky Gervais' literary accomplishments demonstrate his versatility as a creative talent. His ability to engage readers through books, essays, and articles, and his success in the world of comedy writing showcase his skills as a writer beyond the performing arts. Through his literary endeavors, Gervais has further solidified his reputation as a multi-dimensional entertainer and storyteller, leaving a lasting impact on the literary and comedy worlds alike.

Activism and Controversies
Animal Rights Advocacy

Ricky Gervais is a passionate advocate for animal rights and has been actively involved in promoting awareness and change in this area. His advocacy work reflects his commitment to animal welfare and his belief in the importance of compassion and ethical treatment of animals.

Gervais has used his platform and influence to raise awareness about various animal rights issues and to speak out against animal cruelty. He has been vocal in condemning practices such as trophy hunting, fur farming, and animal testing, using his social media presence and public appearances to share information and rally support for change.

One of the organizations that Gervais actively supports is the Humane Society International (HSI), a global animal protection organization. He has collaborated with HSI on campaigns aimed at ending the use of animals in cosmetic testing, promoting the adoption of rescue animals, and raising awareness about wildlife conservation.

Gervais has also used his comedic talents to shed light on animal rights issues through his work. For instance, in his Netflix series "After Life," he explores the bond between humans and animals and addresses themes of empathy and kindness towards animals. By weaving these messages into his storytelling, Gervais has been able to reach a wide audience and provoke thought and discussion on the topic.

In addition to his advocacy work, Gervais has been involved in several initiatives and events supporting animal welfare. He has lent his support to fundraising efforts for animal rescue organizations and has participated in campaigns urging governments to enact stricter laws protecting animals.

While Gervais' animal rights advocacy has garnered widespread support, it has also attracted some controversy. His outspokenness and sharp humor have occasionally resulted in backlash from individuals who hold opposing views. However, Gervais remains undeterred in his efforts to bring attention to animal welfare issues and promote a more compassionate and ethical treatment of animals.

Ricky Gervais' dedication to animal rights advocacy showcases his commitment to making a positive impact beyond the entertainment industry. Through his activism, he has used his platform to raise awareness, challenge societal norms, and promote change in the way animals are treated. His efforts have inspired many and continue to shape conversations surrounding animal rights and welfare.

Controversial Statements and Responses

Ricky Gervais is known for his candid and often controversial statements on a variety of subjects. His outspoken nature and willingness to tackle sensitive topics have garnered both praise and criticism throughout his career. Here are some notable examples of controversial statements made by Gervais and his responses to the ensuing reactions:

- Atheism and Religion:

Gervais is an atheist and has been vocal about his skepticism toward organized religion. His comments and jokes about religion have generated controversy, with some religious groups and individuals taking offense. In response, Gervais has defended his right to free speech and maintained that comedy allows for the questioning of all beliefs and ideologies, including religious ones.

- Transgender Issues:

Gervais has made comments related to transgender issues that have drawn criticism. Some have accused him of making jokes that they deem insensitive or offensive. Gervais has defended his jokes as part of his comedy style, asserting that he aims to challenge societal norms and explore taboo subjects. He has also emphasized the importance of distinguishing between a joke and personal beliefs, stating that he supports transgender rights and equality.

- Controversial Awards Show Monologues:

Gervais has hosted awards shows, such as the Golden Globe Awards, where he has delivered provocative and biting monologues that have garnered mixed reactions. His pointed jabs at celebrities and institutions have been praised by some for their boldness and irreverence, while others have criticized him for being too harsh or crossing the line. Gervais has defended his monologues as a way to hold powerful figures accountable and challenge the notion of excessive self-importance in the entertainment industry.

- Animal Rights Advocacy:

While Gervais' animal rights advocacy has received widespread support, it has also faced criticism from individuals with differing views on the topic. Some have accused him of being too extreme or dismissing cultural practices related to animals. Gervais has maintained his position, emphasizing the importance of compassion and ethical treatment of animals and standing by his efforts to raise awareness and promote change.

In response to controversies surrounding his statements, Gervais has often defended his right to freedom of speech and the role of comedy in questioning societal norms and beliefs. He has emphasized that his intention is not to cause harm or offend but rather to provoke thought and challenge the status quo. Gervais has stated that comedy should not be exempt from scrutiny and that it has the power to explore uncomfortable subjects and spark meaningful conversations.

It is worth noting that while Gervais has received criticism for his controversial statements, he has also garnered a significant following and support from fans who appreciate his unapologetic approach and willingness to address sensitive issues. His ability to spark debate and provoke reactions is a testament to his impact as a comedian and social commentator.

Overall, Ricky Gervais' controversial statements and responses demonstrate his commitment to free expression, his belief in the power of comedy to challenge established ideas, and his willingness to engage in dialogue about important social issues, even when met with disagreement or controversy.

Impact on Public Discourse

Ricky Gervais has had a notable impact on public discourse through his comedy, outspokenness, and willingness to tackle controversial topics. His influence extends beyond the entertainment industry, as he has used his platform to engage in meaningful discussions and challenge societal norms. Here are some ways in which Gervais has made an impact on public discourse:

- Provoking Thought and Discussion:

Gervais' comedy often delves into sensitive subjects and challenges established beliefs. By tackling topics such as religion, atheism, political correctness, and social issues, he sparks thought and encourages dialogue among his audience. Gervais prompts individuals to critically examine their own perspectives, contributing to a more open and engaged public discourse.

- Questioning Authority and Celebrity Culture:

Through his hosting of awards shows and pointed monologues, Gervais has been unafraid to confront celebrities and institutions. He uses his platform to challenge the notion of excessive self-importance, encouraging scrutiny of authority figures and questioning the cult of celebrity. Gervais' irreverent approach has prompted discussions about the role and influence of fame in society.

- Advocating for Freedom of Speech:

Gervais staunchly defends the right to freedom of speech, often emphasizing the importance of open dialogue and the ability to discuss even the most controversial topics. His own willingness to address sensitive subjects has been seen as a powerful example of exercising freedom of expression. Gervais' advocacy for free speech has contributed to ongoing conversations about the limits and boundaries of public discourse.

- Animal Rights and Ethical Treatment of Animals:

As a passionate advocate for animal rights, Gervais has raised awareness and sparked discussions about ethical treatment of animals, animal cruelty, and environmental issues. His outspokenness and support for organizations like the Humane Society International have drawn attention to these topics, encouraging public discourse and inspiring others to get involved.

Impact on Comedy and Social Commentary:
Gervais' unique comedic style, blending humor with insightful social commentary, has influenced a generation of comedians and artists. His ability to address controversial subjects and challenge the status quo has paved the way for more open and honest conversations in comedy. Gervais'

impact on the comedy landscape has contributed to a broader range of voices and perspectives being heard.

While Gervais' approach has garnered both praise and criticism, his influence on public discourse cannot be denied. Through his comedy, advocacy, and willingness to tackle taboo subjects, he has challenged societal norms, promoted critical thinking, and encouraged open dialogue. Ricky Gervais' impact on public discourse serves as a reminder of the power of comedy and the importance of engaging in meaningful conversations about the issues that shape our world.

Chapter 5 Personal Life and Philanthropy

Relationships and Family

Ricky Gervais prefers to keep his personal life relatively private, but there are some aspects of his relationships and family that are known to the public.

Gervais has been in a long-term relationship with Jane Fallon, a British author, television producer, and former radio producer. The couple has been together since the 1980s and has chosen not to marry, stating that they don't feel the need for a legal commitment to validate their relationship. Gervais has often expressed his love and admiration for Fallon, referring to her as his partner and soulmate.

While Gervais and Fallon have chosen not to have children, they are known to be devoted animal lovers and have several pets. They have shared their lives with cats and dogs, and Gervais has frequently posted photos and anecdotes about their furry companions on social media. Their love for animals extends beyond their own pets, as Gervais actively supports animal rights and advocates for their welfare.

Despite their decision not to have children, Gervais has spoken about his fondness for kids and his enjoyment of spending time with his nieces and nephews. He has often mentioned his close relationship with his family and the importance of their support throughout his career.

While Gervais maintains a relatively private personal life, his relationships and family play a significant role in his overall happiness and well-being. His long-term partnership with Jane Fallon and his love for animals reflect important aspects of his personal values and priorities.

Charitable Contributions

Ricky Gervais has been involved in various charitable endeavors and has made notable contributions to philanthropic causes. Here are some examples of his charitable work:

- Animal Rights and Welfare:
Gervais is a passionate advocate for animal rights and has actively supported organizations working to protect and improve the lives of animals. He has

donated both his time and financial resources to charities such as the Humane Society International (HSI) and Animals Asia. Gervais has used his platform to raise awareness about animal cruelty, promote adoption of rescue animals, and campaign against practices like fur farming and trophy hunting.

- Cancer Research:

Gervais has lent his support to cancer research and treatment initiatives. He has participated in fundraising events and campaigns aimed at raising funds for cancer research organizations. Gervais' contributions have helped to advance the fight against cancer and improve the lives of individuals affected by the disease.

- Humanitarian Efforts:

Gervais has shown a commitment to various humanitarian causes. He has supported organizations such as Comic Relief, which works to tackle poverty and social injustices in the UK and around the world. Gervais has also been involved in fundraising efforts for organizations like Save the Children, supporting their work to improve the lives of children in need.

- Mental Health Awareness:

Gervais has been an advocate for mental health awareness and has used his platform to promote understanding and destigmatization of mental health issues. He has spoken openly about his own experiences with depression and has supported initiatives aimed at providing resources and support for individuals facing mental health challenges.

- Stand-up Comedy for Charity:

Gervais has performed in charity stand-up comedy shows, where proceeds from ticket sales are donated to charitable organizations. These performances have helped raise significant funds for causes such as cancer research, poverty alleviation, and animal welfare.

Ricky Gervais' charitable contributions highlight his dedication to making a positive impact beyond his career in entertainment. His support for animal rights, cancer research, humanitarian causes, and mental health awareness reflects his empathy, compassion, and desire to help those in need. Through his philanthropic efforts, Gervais has used his influence to make a difference and inspire others to get involved in charitable endeavors.

Hobbies and Interests

Outside of his professional endeavors, Ricky Gervais has various hobbies and interests that contribute to his well-rounded life. Here are some known hobbies and interests of Ricky Gervais:

- Music:

Gervais is an avid music fan and has expressed his passion for music on numerous occasions. He enjoys listening to a wide range of genres, including rock, pop, and classical music. Gervais has even curated and shared playlists of his favorite songs, showcasing his diverse musical taste.

- Reading:

Gervais is known to be an avid reader and has recommended books on his social media accounts. He has shown an interest in various genres, including fiction, non-fiction, and comedy. Gervais has mentioned authors such as George Orwell, Christopher Hitchens, and Carl Sagan as influences on his thinking and writing.

- Film and Television:

As a creator and actor in the entertainment industry, Gervais has a keen interest in film and television. He has shared his love for movies and TV shows in interviews and social media posts. Gervais appreciates well-crafted storytelling and has expressed admiration for filmmakers and actors who inspire him.

- Nature and Wildlife:

Gervais has shown a deep appreciation for nature and wildlife. He often shares photographs and videos of animals, showcasing his love for the natural world. Gervais has also been involved in campaigns and initiatives supporting wildlife conservation and raising awareness about environmental issues.

- Stand-up Comedy and Live Performances:

Despite being a highly successful comedian and actor, Gervais still enjoys attending stand-up comedy shows and live performances. He appreciates the art of stand-up comedy and has been spotted attending performances of fellow comedians, demonstrating his ongoing interest and support for the comedy community.

- Sports:

While not as prominently discussed as some of his other hobbies, Gervais has shown a casual interest in sports. He has made references to football (soccer) and has occasionally shared his thoughts on sports events through social media.

Rcky Gervais' hobbies and interests showcase his diverse tastes and passions, contributing to his personal fulfillment and influencing various aspects of his life and work.

Legacy and Influence

Cultural Impact and Popularity

Ricky Gervais has left a lasting legacy and has had a significant cultural impact on the entertainment industry and popular culture. His contributions as a comedian, writer, actor, and social commentator have garnered him a dedicated fan base and earned him widespread recognition. Here are some key aspects of Gervais' cultural impact and popularity:

- The Office: Gervais' creation and portrayal of the character David Brent in the British sitcom "The Office" revolutionized the comedy landscape. The show's mockumentary format, naturalistic style, and cringe-worthy humor set a new standard for comedy television. It inspired a wave of similar mockumentary-style shows and influenced a generation of comedians and writers.

- Comedy and Satire: Gervais' comedic style, characterized by sharp wit, observational humor, and willingness to tackle taboo subjects, has had a significant impact on the comedy genre. His ability to blend satire with social commentary has inspired countless comedians and writers, and his influence can be seen in the rise of observational comedy in the early 2000s.

- Global Recognition: Gervais' success has transcended national borders, and he henjoyas gained international recognition for his work. His unique brand of comedy has resonated with audiences around the world, leading to widespread popularity and critical acclaim. Gervais' stand-up comedy tours have sold out venues globally, solidifying his status as a comedic icon.

- Hosting Awards Shows: Gervais' hosting gigs at prestigious awards shows, such as the Golden Globe Awards, have become legendary. His irreverent and fearless approach to hosting has challenged the norms of these events, injecting them with a dose of humor, controversy, and unfiltered commentary. His hosting performances have been both praised and criticized, but they have undeniably left a lasting impact on the awards show landscape.

- Social Commentary and Provoking Debate: Gervais' willingness to address sensitive and controversial topics has made him a prominent figure in public discourse. His comedic material and public statements have sparked conversations, challenged societal norms, and encouraged critical thinking. Gervais' ability to provoke debate and encourage dialogue on important issues has solidified his influence as more than just a comedian.

- Philanthropy and Animal Rights Advocacy: Gervais' dedication to philanthropy, particularly in the areas of animal rights and welfare, has inspired many. His support for organizations and campaigns has raised awareness and contributed to positive change. Gervais' outspokenness on these issues has encouraged others to get involved and make a difference.

Ricky Gervais' cultural impact and popularity stem from his unique comedic talent, fearlessness in tackling controversial subjects, and dedication to social commentary. His influence on the comedy genre, television landscape, and public discourse is evident in the continued relevance of his work and the ongoing discussions sparked by his performances and statements. Gervais' legacy is one of pushing boundaries, challenging the status quo, and using comedy as a vehicle for social critique.

Influence on Comedy and Entertainment

Ricky Gervais has had a significant influence on comedy and entertainment, shaping the landscape and inspiring future generations of comedians and artists. His unique comedic style, unapologetic approach, and willingness to tackle controversial subjects have made a lasting impact. Here are some key aspects of Gervais' influence on comedy and entertainment:

- Mockumentary Format and Naturalistic Comedy: Gervais' groundbreaking work on "The Office" popularized the mockumentary format in comedy television. The show's documentary-style approach, characterized by its realistic portrayal of workplace dynamics and awkward humor, influenced a wave of similar shows, both in the UK and internationally. Gervais' naturalistic comedic style, rooted in everyday observations and relatable situations, has become a hallmark of modern comedy.

- Blurring the Line Between Comedy and Drama: Gervais has demonstrated his ability to seamlessly blend comedy with dramatic elements. His projects often explore serious themes and tackle poignant subjects while maintaining a comedic edge. This blurring of genres has influenced a new wave of comedies that push the boundaries of traditional comedic storytelling, allowing for more nuanced and emotionally resonant narratives.

- Provoking Thought and Challenging Taboos: Gervais' fearlessness in addressing sensitive and taboo subjects has had a profound impact on comedy. He has challenged societal norms, questioned authority, and pushed the boundaries of what is deemed acceptable in comedy. Gervais' ability to tackle controversial topics with intelligence, wit, and insight has inspired other comedians to take risks and engage in more thought-provoking material.

- Influence on Stand-up Comedy: Gervais' success in stand-up comedy has inspired countless comedians around the world. His raw and honest approach to storytelling, coupled with his skillful delivery and mastery of timing, has set a high standard for stand-up comedy. Gervais' influence can be seen in the rise of observational comedy and the trend of comedians using their platforms to share personal stories and tackle social issues.

- Hosting Awards Shows with Irreverence: Gervais' hosting performances at awards shows, characterized by his irreverent humor and fearless takedowns of celebrities and institutions, have left a lasting impact. His unfiltered and often controversial monologues have challenged the norms of these events, injecting them with a refreshing dose of honesty and satire. Gervais' hosting style has inspired other comedians to bring their unique voices and perspectives to awards show hosting.

- Pioneering Direct-to-Consumer Distribution: Gervais has embraced new platforms and distribution models, paving the way for direct-to-consumer content delivery. With projects like "Derek" and "After Life," Gervais has bypassed traditional television networks, opting for platforms like Netflix to reach a global audience. This approach has opened up new opportunities for content creators and disrupted the traditional entertainment industry.

Ricky Gervais' influence on comedy and entertainment is far-reaching and continues to shape the industry. His innovative storytelling, boundary-pushing comedy, and willingness to tackle challenging subjects have inspired comedians, writers, and creators to take risks, challenge conventions, and use comedy as a tool for social commentary. Gervais' impact on the comedy landscape is a testament to his talent, originality, and enduring legacy.

Enduring Legacy

Ricky Gervais has left an enduring legacy in the world of comedy and entertainment. His contributions have shaped the industry and inspired a new generation of comedians, writers, and performers. Here are some key aspects of Gervais' enduring legacy:

- Influential and Iconic Comedic Characters: Gervais' creation and portrayal of iconic characters like David Brent in "The Office" and Andy Millman in "Extras" have become legendary. These characters embody the flaws, insecurities, and complexities of everyday individuals, resonating with audiences on a profound level. Gervais' ability to create relatable and memorable characters has set a high standard for character-driven comedy.

- Impact on Comedy Writing and Style: Gervais' writing style, characterized by sharp wit, observational humor, and a blend of comedy and drama, has had a lasting impact on the comedy landscape. His use of realism, naturalistic dialogue, and willingness to tackle taboo subjects has inspired a new generation of comedy writers to explore more nuanced and authentic storytelling.

- Pioneering Mockumentary Format: Gervais' innovative use of the mockumentary format in "The Office" revolutionized comedy television. The show's documentary-style approach and awkward humor set a new standard for sitcoms, influencing numerous subsequent shows in the genre. The mockumentary format continues to be a popular and effective storytelling technique in comedy.

- Fearlessness and Boundary-Pushing Comedy: Gervais' fearlessness in addressing controversial subjects and challenging societal norms has left a lasting mark on comedy. His ability to provoke thought, challenge taboos, and push the boundaries of what is considered acceptable in comedy has inspired comedians to take risks, engage in social commentary, and use their platforms to spark meaningful conversations.

- Global Reach and International Influence: Gervais' popularity and influence extend far beyond his home country of the United Kingdom. His work has gained international acclaim and has resonated with audiences around the world. Gervais' ability to connect with diverse audiences through his universal themes and relatable humor has solidified his status as a global comedic icon.

- Cultural Impact and Legacy of Shows: Gervais' shows, such as "The Office" and "Extras," continue to be celebrated and referenced in popular culture. Their impact can be seen in the numerous adaptations and spin-offs they have inspired, both in the UK and internationally. Gervais' shows have become touchstones of modern comedy, influencing subsequent generations of comedians and serving as a benchmark for quality storytelling.

- Philanthropic Contributions and Advocacy: Gervais' dedication to philanthropy, particularly in animal rights advocacy and support for charitable causes, has left a lasting impact beyond his comedic work. His efforts to raise awareness, contribute to positive change, and inspire others to get involved have made a tangible difference in the lives of animals and individuals in need.

Ricky Gervais' enduring legacy is a testament to his talent, originality, and fearlessness in challenging conventions and pushing the boundaries of comedy. His impact on the comedy landscape, television industry, and social commentary continues to be felt, and his work will be celebrated for generations to come.

Printed in Great Britain
by Amazon